When2Pray

When2Pray

Barrie & Eileen Jones

One Accord

Published by RoperPenberthy Publishing Ltd
PO Box 545, Horsham, England

Text copyright © Barrie & Eileen Jones

All Bible quotations are from the New International Version,
unless otherwise stated

First published in 2004

ISBN 1 903905 14 1

Cover design by Angie Moyler

Typeset by Avocet Typeset, Chilton, Aylesbury, Bucks
Printed in the United Kingdom by Bell and Bain Ltd

ACKNOWLEDGEMENTS

Thanks to all who have encouraged us and prayed for this book. The vision for thousands of couples praying and the book first came from John Kerr, Director of *One Accord*.

Our warmest thanks go to the many couples who contributed their personal experiences of learning to pray together. All your stories have enriched the whole.

We're very grateful to those who took the time to comment so usefully and positively on the manuscript.

Jim Penberthy and Angie Moyler at RoperPenberthy Publishing have been a source of great encouragement to us.

F O R E W O R D

When we pray together as a married couple, we discover more about God and his love for each one of us – but we also discover more about our husband or wife. As we do this, the result can only draw us closer together. Prayer becomes like 'glue' in our relationship. Statistics bear this out. One survey revealed that, while the national average of marriage breakdown is two out of every five marriages, for couples who pray together on a regular basis, the figure is more like one in every four hundred.

Barrie and Eileen write out of their experience of the difference that praying together has made in their marriage of thirty-eight years. This book will help couples to get started, encourage them to keep going and, most of all, inspire them to believe that praying together will make a difference.

Our hope and prayer is that *When2Pray* will cause thousands of couples to imitate them, for not only will their own relationship be immeasurably strengthened, but countless others will be the beneficiaries of their joint prayers.

Nicky and Sila Lee

WHEN TWO PRAY

Introduction

But Jesus said, "Not everyone is mature enough to live a married life. It requires a certain aptitude and grace. Marriage isn't for everyone . . . But if you are capable of growing into the largeness of marriage, do it." (TM Matt.19:11-12)

The aim of this simple book is to . . .

➢ help couples to pray together for the first time

➢ encourage couples who've stopped to start again, and

➢ inspire those already praying together

What Barrie and I have written comes out of our own lives and from the experiences of many other couples who, from their own journeys in prayer, have opened up to us the lessons they have learnt.

Wind of change

Just when we'd been married for 20 years, we went away on a marriage enrichment course. Until then we certainly thought we were happily married . . . but the experience of that weekend blew a searching wind of change right through our relationship. Unknown windows and doors of communication opened between us, with the unexpected effect of increasing our sense of security, as well as giving us a greater delight and an expectation of growth in our love for one another.

Thinking about it later, Barrie realised that he had seen our life together as having arrived at a pleasant plateau! From that time on, he'd imagined, we would meander contentedly along together into the sunset of life . . . with nothing much changing. But the truth hit him like a bombshell . . . any living thing, including a marriage relationship, which is not actively cared for does not stay the same but begins to wither. On the other hand, he saw the prospect of growing into the *largeness of marriage* as a glorious promise. And so together we responded to the invitation to plunge wholeheartedly into our marriage and to give our relationship the top priority in our lives.

Praying together has always been important to us even though we've often needed a fresh kick-start to keep it going, but the impact of the marriage course really did help us open our hearts to one another as well as increase our keenness to pray together.

Since then, throughout our 18 years experience of marriage ministry through *Marriage Review* (now *One Accord),* we have met many couples who want to pray together but don't, as well as many others who have stopped praying because of the pressures of life and who desperately want to restart.

So you can be sure you are not the only ones who have hit barriers trying to get time for prayer established in your lives.

As you read on you may recognise some of the early 'praying together' embarrassments and awkwardnesses that others have felt . . . and we hope you will be encouraged to see how breaking through the barriers brings many benefits!

WHEN2PRAY

Let other people's experiences become stepping stones to help YOU launch into what at first may feel a strange activity but, with trust and faith, can deepen your relationship with God and with your marriage partner.

CHAPTER ONE

THE CHALLENGE

Prayer can be difficult and for some the thought of praying with their husband or wife is completely daunting. At a session of *The Marriage Course* produced by Holy Trinity Church, Brompton, a woman told the leaders that "She would rather run down the road naked than pray with her husband!" Friends of ours admitted that when they first started praying together, they could only do it with the lights out! That's just how embarrassing the idea of praying as a couple can be for some!

A first response for couples when the subject of praying together comes up, is to feel defensive about their marriage and the quality of their relationship. "We're OK," they say. Perhaps they don't want to rock the boat. Well . . . maybe God does!

> *Marriage is not about the joining of two lives but the abandoning of two lives that one new one may begin.*
> Mike Mason

For those who have not prayed out loud together before, it can seem difficult. If you're newly married or brand new Christians, the whole idea of making yourself vulnerable to one another by expressing 'private' thoughts and prayers can definitely feel a step too far.

Getting started

We had spent so little time together in our 18 month engagement, because Barrie was in a ship in the Far East most of that time, that I wasn't even sure whether or not he took sugar in his tea! What we were sure about was that we didn't just want to be two Christians who were married. We wanted a Christian marriage, one where God was at the centre. So we started to pray together . . . gritting our teeth and keeping going through the embarrassment and awkwardness I certainly felt as we began.

The thing that made all the difference to us was an agreement that . . . if one of us suggested a time of prayer or Bible reading, the other would not refuse.

The other *might* say, "Just give me five minutes to finish this" but would not say, "*No*". As we look back we can see this was the gold brick in the foundations we laid, helping us to grow without fear of rejection, in confidence with God and each other.

Restoration

So why should the idea of sharing prayer raise so many barriers in our minds?

One reason may be the very thought of inviting your partner into your private conversations with God. If you have a precious and well-established personal prayer time yourself, you may especially feel there's no need to pray together.

Perhaps there is a reason that is a little more fundamental than that though . . . something which has everything to do with the coming of sin into the world?

THE CHALLENGE

Before the time when they flouted God's authority, Adam and Eve clearly had a spiritual oneness with each other and a loving companionship with God that was brutally broken when that fatal choice to disobey was made.

God's mournful cry of, "Adam . . . where are you?" (Genesis 3:9) rings its lament down the ages . . . proclaiming the awful separation from God that sin brings.

But (a huge but!) just as Jesus brought full reconciliation – redemption – to mankind through his death upon the cross, so marriage was redeemed at the same time and by the same astonishing grace!

The wonderful news is that the spiritual brokenness and inhibition between *us-and-God-and-each-other* has been dealt with and we can start to claim back, with utmost confidence, a restored unity in prayer.

So, even though it is often not simple . . . natural . . . or, easy, every time a husband and wife pray together they celebrate the fact that included in the redemption of humankind was *their* marriage relationship!

Keep going!

As my husband, Barrie, and I introduce ourselves to you through this book, we have to say that in no way have we been 'pray-ers together' throughout *every* part of 38 years of our married life. We have often needed to renew our determination to spend that time together. What we can say is that praying together has been, and continues to be, a great strength and blessing. Through the years we've been given comfort, endurance, healing and answers. Answers, fascinatingly, that often arrive in form or solution very different to our expectations.

Being able to pray together has made such a big contribution to the satisfying intimacy and communication we, and many others experience, that we want to encourage more and more couples to step out in prayer . . .

> ➢ for our own and other marriages

> ➢ for our churches, communities and work places, and

> ➢ for our nation

In fact, in something of a new way, we believe the Holy Spirit is calling *thousands* of married couples to start praying together for the sake of marriage.

If most of us find praying together difficult at the beginning, maybe there's a message here, because perhaps we're standing on the threshold of something important?

So, the message of this small book is . . .

> ➢ Think BIG!

> ➢ Start small . . . but start!

CHAPTER TWO

WHY PRAY TOGETHER?

In our marriage . . . *"To whom should we go, Lord? You alone have the words that give eternal life."* (John 6:68)

Two together in relationship with God was His first intention and, as we've said, this was what He was looking for in the beginning. The pleasure to God of the trust and simplicity enjoyed in that early relationship is clear and remains a compelling model for us.

If, as the years go by, we want our marriage to become *something beautiful for God* and operate as a sign of God's love in the world, it can only happen through our willingness to be open to and dependent on Him.

What better way to mature and beautify our marriage than through our influence on each other, as this descriptive image . . . "As iron sharpens iron, so one person sharpens another." (Proverbs 27: 17) suggests to us. I recognise that Barrie's much more loving response to issues has often challenged my negative feelings of selfishness or pride as we've prayed together.

Our close friends, Richard and Rosalyn Dean, speaking from

their experience, say, . . . *"We both know that praying together is life giving and it works!"*

Why pray together? Because when we do we are strengthened and blessed. When God is central to our lives, we can bring his peace and presence to others. When we pray together we have the promise of Jesus . . . "When two of you get together on anything at all on earth and make a prayer of it, my Father in heaven goes into action. And when two or three of you are together because of me, you can be sure that I'll be there." (Matt 18:19,20 The Message)

Equal status

The nature of our *designed-for-each-other* relationship is made very plain in Genesis 1:27, "So God created people in his own image; God patterned them after himself; male and female he created them."

This key principle of marriage proclaims that men and women are of equal value, because both are made in God's image, though wonderfully different. Although in the early church women were treated as equal to men, through Roman and Greek influences this understanding was quickly lost and it has taken almost 2000 years for the church to regain it.

We need be in no doubt that the consequences of that disastrous rift from God, expressed in those often misused words . . . "Your husband shall rule over you." (RSV Genesis 3:16) was swept away by the Cross. Through the death of Jesus our relationship with God was restored and each of us has been given the grace and possibility to live out God's *original* design and plan for marriage.

Like two children coming to Father, we're both free to take part in an activity of equals, and in that unity we're released to bring our concerns, crises and joys of daily life to Him.

> *My most brilliant achievement was my ability to be able to persuade my wife to marry me.*
> Winston Churchill

Standing against the flow

The late Cardinal Basil Hume once said that Christian marriages and families are called to be a 'sign of contradiction to the world'.

Couples who practise praying together are allowing Jesus to have the chance of guiding, comforting and inspiring their lives. What better way to know the character of God, to be able to teach our children and draw on His wisdom for living, than by reading the Bible and praying together?

As His church we need eyes wide open to the spiritual poverty we see all around us, so that we can help meet the fallout from our increasingly desperate post-modern society. Right here and now, as we pray in unity, we can be one of the ways through which God will bring change. We can become part of an effective, salty edge of dissent in society, offering an alternative hope – through Christ.

An essential oil

Praying together helps harmony in the home! It's very difficult to pray if there is any resentment or anger between us. If we allow the soothing *essential oil* of forgiveness to flow between us, we are much more able to keep short accounts and to be kind to one another. Exercising forgiveness means that the way is cleared for us to pray together. "How wonderful, how pleasant when people get along! It's like costly anointing oil flowing down head and beard." (TM Psalm 133:1) . . . and there's more! The Psalm goes on to tell us that, when this sort of positive atmosphere prevails, God gives his blessing.

So forgiveness between us is clearly an activity of equality! If we are both willing to bless and forgive, no barriers to communication will be able to build up between either ourselves or with God.

Close friends from our time in the Royal Navy, told us that for them . . .

> *"A lovely by-product of praying together is that it has helped prevent us nursing resentment and other negative feelings towards one another."*

As all married couples know, because we are fallible human beings, close living demands that we make sure there is a healthy inter-flow of forgiveness between us.

Peter Ustinov, the veteran actor and author, put it this way . . .

> *"Love is an endless act of forgiveness."*

But it may be costly!

Walking in openness together may be costly but it is also the key to blessing. Too many of us are hindered from reaching out to a needy world because family relationships are incapacitated and wounded. Instead of being able to serve God together, we find all our energies and strengths are engaged in just trying to hold our own lives together.

Life happens! So we'll be very unusual if we haven't had to struggle with issues that have caused wounds both from within the family and from without. But the fundamental truth is that individuals or couples will be quite useless unless they become active *'forgivers'*.

It may take some getting there but unless we can arrive at a place where we are able to say, "Lord, I want to forgive everybody for everything, help me let go of all bitterness and resentment", nothing will change.

> Jesus warned, *"And when you stand praying, if you hold anything against anyone, forgive him, so that your Father in heaven may forgive your sins"*. (Mark 11:25)

So as a preliminary step, let's take time to check if we are holding 'anything against anyone' right now. When we gave our lives to Jesus everything changed, ALL our sin was forgiven! The least we can do is to forgive those who have hurt us, because unity represents God's heart. On the other hand, the devil's aim is to stir up as much disunity as possible, whether that's at work, in the church or in our homes. Let's dare to walk in the light together, bringing wounds, anger, hurts, sulks into the open, so that they can no longer harm our marriage or our relationship with God.

Positive action

Peter reminds us that, "Our prayers are hindered if we are not treating each other well." (1Peter 3:7)

Let's work at being generous towards one another, because giving affirming love in small gestures helps create unity and strength. Sometimes a loving gesture may not be the result of 'feelings' but may purely be an act of the will. A friend, whose marriage was plummeting in a downward spiral, took her husband's favourite cream trousers to the cleaners as a conscious act of love. The recovery of their feelings for each other began from that moment.

I have never forgotten a teenage girl from a Christian family saying in a youth group discussion, "What's so good about marriage anyway? I don't want to end up like my mum and dad!"

Taking care of our marriage relationship and giving time to each other makes sense, because disunity and conflict give off a bad smell . . . nobody wants to get too close!

But, as we all know, the fragrance and witness of a couple putting each other first is irresistible.

In a preface to his extraordinary book *The Mystery of Marriage*, Mike Mason, says

"I believe that couples who submit wholeheartedly in marriage both to God and to one another, stand on the threshold of Paradise, of pure bliss."

Pure bliss is within our grasp as we put the other first! Then comes the reward, as the years go by . . . *our* marriage, *our* love and faithfulness becoming a well from which many may draw.

What about the children?

Learning to pray together will bless our children – whatever their age!

WHY PRAY TOGETHER?

From our experience we know that children don't expect their parents to be perfect. That's a relief! But what they do expect is to see them *honestly* and *practically* doing their best (how ever feebly) to live out the Christian faith they *say* they believe. As parents we have the enormous privilege of rising to that challenge. It's very hard for kids to hear the Truth if they don't see parents being real and, at some time in the day, depending on God through prayer and Bible reading.

God's faithfulness

"Our hearts desire is to bring our young 'close to the altar". (Psalm 84:3)

If this verse expresses our 'heart's desire' then, from the experience of others, we can be sure of His faithfulness. Some have prayed like this . . .

- *God gave strength and wisdom to a couple who fasted just one evening a week for their children during their teenage years. All their children now love and serve the Lord.*

- *Regular prayers by another couple for good relationships with their adult sons, daughter and son-in-law are being fully answered.*

- *Canadian author, Mike Mason and his wife Karen, pray together nightly with their teenage daughter in a ritual that has become very important to them.*

- *Grandparents with a large tally of grandchildren are currently praying for the future husbands/wives of them all.*

- *A Mum spends the 7 minutes it takes to walk back from dropping her daughter off at school, praying specifically for each of her children.*

- *Parents of four have found that laying hands on their children and praying over them while they are asleep – particularly if they've been cross with them, or if they're really struggling with something – makes a big difference.*

- *Through rebellious teen years, a Mum found strength and encouragement through praising God and praying in her child's bedroom – while he was at school.*

By praying together for our children and grandchildren we are being faithful to ask . . . and God will be faithful to answer.

When we experience grief

The Bible describes our Father God as '*the Father of mercies and God of all comfort, who comforts us in all our afflictions.*' (2 Cor 1:3,4) These verses display God's desire to meet with us in sorrow but we know that the grief and pain that life sometimes brings can either draw a couple closer together – or it can drive them apart.

If a regular habit of praying together is in place, and we've been able to share pain and failures together, that very vulnerability builds a strong foundation of trust between us. A couple's past unity and comradeship can continue to give strength, even though some find praying goes out of the window for a while, as they work through the process of grieving.

A pastor and his wife told us they found their habit of praying together was '*an absolutely vital support*' to them, throughout a chemotherapy course for breast cancer.

WHY PRAY TOGETHER?

Some friends who are deeply involved in ministry to marriage, and who experienced the agony of losing their adult son in a car accident found that . . .

"In the shocking aftermath of Stuart's death, prayer was a great comfort but difficulties set in with normal grief reactions. We didn't lose relationship with a Father who loves us, but somehow prayer as a whole was called into question when one of the people we had prayed for most was suddenly gone in dreadful circumstances.

Our relationship, with God and each other, might not have survived the battering if we had not already been on a journey of building intimacy in the good times in preparation for the bad.

We struggled with our own expectations, and sometimes those of others, of how we "should" be. Fortunately, God places no such expectations upon us. A friend sent us this helpful paraphrase of some words of Jesus, "Give me your unbearably heavy weight of this circumstance and I will bear it for you, rest in my arms and let me carry you through this time." So, we hold onto God's truth – and wait for our feelings to follow."

When trauma and sadness come into our lives we naturally cry out to God. Even as we pray we're aware that things cannot always be put right because human choices and evil forces have their role to play. Jesus prayed in the Garden of Gethsemane to be relieved of the terrible burden laid on Him, before He chose to surrender Himself completely to the consequences of mankind's sin.

Many find that reading together the Bible passages that tell out the story of the suffering of Jesus in his life and death, is a very helpful starting point of prayer.

WHEN2PRAY

The power of Christ's suffering to bring comfort is described in this meditation on the scars of Jesus, written just after the end of the First World War by Edward Shillito . . .

Jesus of the Scars
If we have never sought, we seek you now
Your eyes burn through the dark, our only stars
We must have sight of thorn-marks on your brow
We must have you, O Jesus of the scars

The other gods were strong, but you were weak
They rode, but you did stumble to a throne
But to our wounds only God's wounds can speak
And not a god has wounds, but you alone.

CHAPTER THREE

BREAKING THE PRAYER BARRIER

Imagine Jesus standing in front of us, looking straight at us with smiling eyes full of tenderness and searching love, asking us, *"Do you want to be healed?"*

Jesus asked that of a man who had hardly moved for 38 years (John 5:6). What about us? Is our relationship with *God-and-each-other* paralysed too? It's not uncommon.

The fact of the matter is that it's more than possible to recognise a problem and even speak about it frequently but still not be prepared to do anything about it. As we think about our relationship as a couple – can we dare to ask the question, how much have we moved *or* grown towards each other in the last five years?

Taking off the masks

An issue may be difficult, even painful to confront, but think of the wonderful relief when we can at last take off the super-spiritual, super-complacent, super-dishonest masks we wear so readily, even towards our beloved husband or wife.

A person may say,"*Of course, I can't pray with my husband (or wife) . . . it's just impossible!*"

Is it? Before we can begin to move and grow in prayer we might well need to allow God to check out our attitudes.

It's possible, for example, that . . .

> ➤ A superior 'preachy' authority in prayer towards the other is the barrier between us.

> ➤ An overwhelming super-spiritual attitude is undermining the confidence of our husband or wife.

> ➤ We're feeling we don't match up to the textbook standards for praying together and think we're the only ones with this problem.

> ➤ We're just feeling shy and lacking confidence.

> ➤ We've had a row, or we're feeling resentful and angry towards our partner.

> ➤ We haven't seen the importance of praying together, or been challenged to try.

How is it we can make love to each other, but find it so hard to pray together? Is it because in praying together we're opening up our relationship with the Lord (the deepest most intimate part of ourselves) for our partner to see – and this makes us so vulnerable?

We know that even raising the subject of praying with a husband or wife can take courage, because we are all fragile in some area or other and each can be quickly wounded by even small rejections. If a hunger to pray together is starting to build in you, pray for this to grow in the other too.

But here's an important reality check . . . we can't *require* another person to change! We just have to be willing to allow the Holy Spirit to change *our* attitudes first and rely on Him to do the same for our partner.

A story

John and Hazel Kerr's story is that . . .

"After we'd been on a marriage course, we decided to give praying together a go for one week. To our astonishment the ceiling did not fall in and we survived. It was not easy but as we had children the family was a natural thing to pray about. The week stretched out and we began to be much happier with each other. Learning to overcome our irritations with the way the other prayed was the next challenge! Hazel felt John's prayers were too long; John thought Hazel's were feebly short and practical (we've since learnt that Hazel's are much nearer the mark).

We thought we should be able to hear God together as a couple. So we began to spend some time separately looking at our Bible notes for the day, then met afterwards to quickly share anything that had occurred to us and then pray. We began to experience a difference.

As time went on our prayer time fell away – Hazel was stretched with the demands of a young family and part-time work and John was working late, so how could they possibly find time for this? One day as he was rehearsing this to God for the umpteenth time, some thoughts came into his mind, "Did he think it was important if they went to bed 15 or 20 minutes later?" Answer, "No". "So what's the big deal about getting up earlier?" That did it and we got our praying off the ground again.

Over the years the freshness and enthusiasm has varied considerably but we cannot now imagine life without praying together.

Our story is this: from a very reluctant and rocky start, we have come to find the person we most want to pray with is each other and we believe it is one of the most important things we do!"

Men and women are different!

Recent books on marriage with titles like *Men are from Mars and Women are from Venus* and *Why Men Don't Listen and Women can't read Maps* are teaching and celebrating the very real differences between the sexes in the emotional, sexual and physical realms. So can we now acknowledge that there might be a difference between the way men and women approach prayer?

For example there is often a natural spirituality in women, which is shown in a readiness to pray and to respond to an invitation to pray. For many men, this sort of response will need much more to be *an act of the will!*

In general terms the male is more likely to focus on the rational and the end result, which perfectly complements the more intuitive/acting from the heart response of the female. We each contribute to a perfect balance *if* we learn to lovingly accept our differences.

It's official! "Men's brains do not notice dust", says social scientist Michael Gurian. "Male and female brains are different and scientists now have the technology to prove it!"

Voyages of discovery

Feeling threatened or defensive about the whole idea of praying together is normal, because it's very easy to think, "I'm not as 'holy' or 'mature' as he/she is". Or, "You pray so differently to me".

Even hearing the other having an intimate relationship with God can be challenging and undermining for some people. If this is true for you, spill the beans! Be honest. And try to talk about your reluctance to pray.

A wife was absolutely amazed to discover her husband felt inadequate because he saw her as being much more mature, though she didn't *see herself* as very mature *or* holy at all! So reckon any increase of honesty between you as a bonus and a step towards discovering a pattern of praying that works for both of you.

Dave and Liz Percival (founders of the unique marriage support website www.2-in-2-1.co.uk) know about that process. This was Dave's experience . . .

"I wanted us to pray together but felt small and incapable – inadequate to reach her standards.

Then a small prayer group started and I felt able to pray with them. As my confidence grew I realised that I didn't necessarily hear from the Lord in words . . . instead I saw pictures – crazy, mixed up scenes like in a dream, yet usually with a message or a theme.

I felt scared to share this with Liz – surely she'd just laugh. Taking my courage in my hands, I asked Liz to just listen and accept it as a gift – not to prod or poke. In the gentleness of Liz's acceptance of me, I started to share these pictures.

We have such starkly different styles – Liz will be given words, perhaps a scripture . . . I will see a picture – not even a logical or rational picture. Sometimes I will describe it to Liz and its meaning will become clear, other times it will seemingly be nothing, yet if I dwell on it, give it time to soak, then gradually the Lord shows me more till His meaning is clear."

Daring to be open and vulnerable with each other has allowed Dave and Liz to move on in intimacy and satisfying (not perfect) prayer together.

Writing a letter may help! If you're finding it too hard to put your feelings into words, many husbands and wives have found expressing their thoughts and feelings in writing has pushed open the door of understanding between them.

One thing you can be sure of is, because prayer is such a hard thing to do, *very few* feel 'good at it'. Even the greatest saints!

Attitudes that help

> Couple prayer is a three –cornered conversation between people who love each other, the more natural our prayers the more real Jesus will become to us.

the
WHEN 2 PRAY
initiative

Matthew 18:19, The Message

Jesus said;
"When two of you
get together on
anything at all
on earth and make
a prayer of it,
my Father in heaven
goes into action"

the
WHEN 2 PRAY
initiative

Matthew 18:19, The Message

Jesus said;
"When two of you
get together on
anything at all
on earth and make
a prayer of it,
my Father in heaven
goes into action"

GOD WANTS THE BEST FOR YOU AND YOUR FAMILY

marriage is under threat

*will you commit
to pray together regularly
for your own marriage and
for other married couples?
join this national initiative now
and begin to*

MAKE A DIFFERENCE

encourage others to join the initiative

*order more copies of this bookmark
and the book by mail order,
in bookshops or from
www.2-in-2-1.co.uk*

oneAccord
strengthening marriage & personal relationships

Market Square, Petworth,
West Sussex GU28 OAH
Tel: 01789 345222
Email: admin@oneaccord.org.uk
www.oneaccord.org.uk

GOD WANTS THE BEST FOR YOU AND YOUR FAMILY

marriage is under threat

*will you commit
to pray together regularly
for your own marriage and
for other married couples?
join this national initiative now
and begin to*

MAKE A DIFFERENCE

encourage others to join the initiative

*order more copies of this bookmark
and the book by mail order,
in bookshops or from
www.2-in-2-1.co.uk*

oneAccord
strengthening marriage & personal relationships

Market Square, Petworth,
West Sussex GU28 OAH
Tel: 01789 345222
Email: admin@oneaccord.org.uk
www.oneaccord.org.uk

GOD WANTS THE BEST FOR YOU AND YOUR FAMILY

marriage is under threat

*will you commit
to pray together regularly
for your own marriage and
for other married couples?
join this national initiative now
and begin to*

MAKE A DIFFERENCE

encourage others to join the initiative

*order more copies of this bookmark
and the book by mail order,
in bookshops or from
www.2-in-2-1.co.uk*

oneAccord
strengthening marriage & personal relationships

Market Square, Petworth,
West Sussex GU28 OAH
Tel; 01789 345222
Email: admin@oneaccord.org.uk
www.oneaccord.org.uk

GOD WANTS THE BEST FOR YOU AND YOUR FAMILY

marriage is under threat

*will you commit
to pray together regularly
for your own marriage and
for other married couples?
join this national initiative now
and begin to*

MAKE A DIFFERENCE

encourage others to join the initiative

*order more copies of this bookmark
and the book by mail order,
in bookshops or from
www.2-in-2-1.co.uk*

oneAccord
strengthening marriage & personal relationships

Market Square, Petworth,
West Sussex GU28 OAH
Tel; 01789 345222
Email: admin@oneaccord.org.uk
www.oneaccord.org.uk

the
WHEN 2 PRAY
initiative

the
WHEN 2 PRAY
initiative

Matthew 18:19, The Message

Jesus said;

"When two of you
get together on
anything at all
on earth and make
a prayer of it,
my Father in heaven
goes into action"

Matthew 18:19, The Message

Jesus said;

"When two of you
get together on
anything at all
on earth and make
a prayer of it,
my Father in heaven
goes into action"

BREAKING THE PRAYER BARRIER

- ➤ Don't start out by trying to impress the other one!

- ➤ Make an agreement not to refuse a suggested time of prayer.

- ➤ Pray as you can – just be yourselves.

- ➤ Allow for the uniqueness of the 'other', and take into account how different the spiritual journey of your husband or wife may have been from your own. Stand in their shoes.

- ➤ Be flexible – relax.

- ➤ Be patient with each other.

- ➤ Remember, praying together is not an entrance exam to Heaven!

- ➤ Try to find a regular agreed time together.

- ➤ Chill out, laugh and keep starting again.

- ➤ Don't use a 'preachy voice'.

- ➤ Disconnect the phone.

- ➤ Don't give up.

This is how others got started . . .

"We found praying aloud together at first easier when we were out walking our dog . . . "

"Because we became Christians after we married, praying together was very strange. We started by sitting side by side and each praying silently . . . then, saying a sentence out loud now and again led us on to feeling comfortable about starting to pray together."

"One day, we decided not to be shy and to find the confidence."

"We just agreed to do it."

"We began by saying grace and then by extending those prayers."

"We started by having a cup of tea first thing, reading a short passage from the Bible and then praying together."

"There came a time when we started to pray . . . just the two of us, shyly, awkwardly, but real."

Michael and Gillian Warren, generous hosts and leaders of many marriage enrichment weekends, say "If you're more used to written prayers, use them or write your own and pray them aloud when you're together . . . gradually you will feel able to add a sentence of your own and it will become easier."

A young naval officer habitually prayed a long grace before his breakfast. One morning his eggs and bacon disappeared, in its place he found a note that said, "WATCH **AND PRAY**"!

Spiritual Barriers

It's helpful to be reminded that . . .

"We are not contending against flesh and blood, but against the principalities, against the powers, against the world rulers of this present darkness, against the spiritual hosts of wickedness in the heavenly places." (Ephesians 6:12).

In some way or other in our daily lives, we all come face to face with spiritual warfare. Some experience spiritual discouragement and feelings of condemnation and the warfare can be intense. Certainly any involvement in the occult makes it difficult to pray, so getting help is a priority. A young couple told us that as they tried to pray together after their marriage, the wife felt overwhelmed with the desire to punch her new husband! Wow! Very alarming for them both. The symptoms varied in intensity so they tried to persevere but eventually confided in an older friend at church. They were prayed for and after this they weren't troubled any more and have been able to grow in their prayer life together.

Accepting one another

It's important to make sure we don't find ourselves being manipulative or starting to pray 'at' each other, or use it as the chance to have a 'dig' at the other one under a *spiritual* veneer, e.g. "*And Lord please help him to get on with things!*"

Carey Moore and Pamela Rosewell Moore, in their encouraging book *What Happens When Husbands and Wives Pray Together*, include the comments of a couple who found their ability to pray together took off after they *accepted* one another.

"They found they needed to tell one another that each accepted the other's prayers. By making a deliberate decision of acceptance, they freed each other of any need to impress their partner.

'This self-consciousness no longer exists now that we both accept each other's prayers."

... That is why marriage is so much more more
interesting than divorce,
Because it's the only known example of the happy
meeting of the immovable object and the irresistible
force ...
Ogden Nash

CHAPTER FOUR

HOW OTHERS PRAY

God's invitation to us is 'seek my face'
(Psalm 27:8).

As we accept this invitation we have his promise that we will *find*
him. Because he is faithful to his word he will respond to our
approach.

Take time to tune into God's heart, approach him with joy, allow
his graciousness and gentleness to open your eyes, to rearrange
your priorities and to change you.

We asked other couples about their prayer times and here are
some of their replies . . .

*"We use the Anglican Morning Prayer before long car journeys
. . . "O Lord, who has safely brought us to the beginning of this
day, defend us in the same by your mighty power . . . "*

"Praying through the Lord's Prayer helped us get started"

*"Reading The Father's Love Letter (see page 56) has helped us
express our thankfulness to God. At first praying together felt
embarrassing but it doesn't at all now and it really feels as*

though we have missed out on an important event in the day if we don't get round to praying together."

"A marriage enrichment weekend we went on gave us a 'kick-start' to our prayer life together'."

"We make creative use of liturgy, prayer books, and offices of morning and evening prayer, compline etc. and the Bible reading notes 'Every Day with Jesus".

"Each day we have ring-fenced time to pray together."

"First thing in the morning in bed together, we like to thank the Lord and acknowledge His Presence with us and commit the day and one another into His Hands. It helps to be aware of the fact that Father is waiting and loves to hear from us."

"We pray at breakfast (including family)."

"When travelling to work together we pray most days."

"We find it more difficult if we don't fit praying together into the first part of the day – it can get put aside. It's been very difficult to pray together with the constant demands of young children and we have experienced a few peaks and troughs in our efforts."

"We find a fairly structured approach helpful. We begin with a Bible reading, this is followed by reflections in prayer on what we have just read before we praise God for who he is and all his blessings."

"Our daily prayer time is built around a weekly prayer diary and seven daily prayer sheets."

HOW OTHERS PRAY

"We set it as a goal during our engagement and he was faithful to lead and make it part of our daily routine – even when he has to rustle me out of bed and I pray reluctantly in a sleepy manner. It's very important to us. He is the morning and I am the night bird! Now we are much more on the same perch!"

"We sing a worship song and then take it in turns to pray for each other and our children and the current concerns."

"We were constant for the first 2-3 years until our daughter was born. After that it has become harder."

"We have continued praying with the children but less together."

"We have built a definite time for prayer into our day."

"We pray together daily over a cup of tea, about 5pm."

"When he has an early morning start or we are apart, he will phone me to pray and it works well. It's become an important part of our life and helps us to stay close not only to each other but also to God."

"We read Operation World together daily and pray for the nations."

"We use a few minutes silence together to listen to God and prepare our hearts and minds for the day."

"We have made a definite decision to cultivate 'an attitude of gratitude' and to speak out our thankfulness to God in our prayer time together."

"We pray for each other's day."

WHEN2PRAY

"We purposely limit praying together to 10 minutes."

These comments are very helpful and represent a huge variety of experience from marriages that have, no doubt, faced similar challenges to our own.

Mike & Kathy Morris have helped many to start to pray and share together through their well-loved book Praying Together. (Now published by Kingsway and incorporated into 'Classics in Prayer'). The book encourages couples to start by saying the Lord's Prayer out loud together and then to take it in turn to say each line. Many have used this idea as a first stepping-stone in getting used to the whole idea of praying together.

Of course it's a fact that different seasons of life make praying together harder to achieve but it is also true that self-discipline and determination are always needed to make it happen. Christianity is above all a message of 'new beginnings' and the area of praying as a couple is no exception to that grace. Honesty compels many of the husbands and wives who have shared their experiences of praying together, to say . . . *don't give up and, if you do, start again!*

CHAPTER FIVE

MAKING IT TOP PRIORITY

'. . . that in everything he may have the pre-eminence' (Col.1: 18)

The evangelist J John and his wife Killy went to the village church near their hotel for Holy Communion at 8am – on the morning after their wedding. They started as they meant to go on . . . and they say, *"Our love of Jesus compels us to pray together."* Twenty years later they are still praying together!

Whatever our age, whether we have children or not, with hectic working lives or retired, we would probably all have to agree that *there is never enough time!*

When you picked up this book you may have thought . . . have our own personal time with God AND find time to pray with our husband or wife? You can't be serious!

Hang on! Do you think then that every couple that pray together live lives of limitless leisure? Surely not!

Isn't it more likely to be true that they have both decided to make praying together a priority in their day – and it happens! Not 365 days in the year . . . not a perfect daily record . . . but regular prayer together takes place.

And the two shall become one . . .

Paul compares the relationship of Jesus Christ and the church with a man and woman's relationship in marriage.

Husbands are called to *"love their wives, as Christ loved the church and gave himself up for her, that he might sanctify her, having cleansed her by the washing of water with the word, that he might present the church to himself radiant . . . that she might be holy and without blemish."* (Ephesians 5.25, 26)

As a man considers these verses, he could ask himself, "as a result of my loving and giving to our relationship, how radiant is my wife?" It has been said that when you look at the face of a man's wife, you will see everything he has invested or withheld.

If his wife could not be described as 'radiant', a husband might take a decision to listen to his wife about her life and aspirations; could try to express affection through giving time to their relationship for fun and relaxation, as well as suggesting that they pray together.

Surprisingly, this same passage in Ephesians urges wives to respond by showing *'respect for their husbands'*, not as we might expect to offer *love* in return. The truth is that most men would say that they feel loved when they *feel* respected.

Understanding this might lead a woman to ask herself, "Is there an atmosphere of respect for my husband in our home?"

Leadership

In one week recently I spoke to a vicar and to a young man who has only been a Christian for 2-3 years. Both men said, "It seems so much easier for women – they want to pray so much more often!"

Paradoxically, in God's economy it is the husband, the one often less *naturally* inclined, who is given a greater responsibility to encourage and lead couple prayer. It's puzzling but at least it means a man has to lean on God rather than on his own natural inclinations.

It is Jesus himself who underlines God's creative intention for men and women, by reminding his disciples . . . "Have you not read that he who made them from the beginning, made them male and female, and said, for this reason a man shall leave his father and mother and be joined to his wife and the two shall become one," (Matt 19:5).

In this way marriage is presented to us as a fantastically high calling right in line with His central purpose. And within that plan each married couple is given an invitation to be involved in the most challenging, most fulfilling lifestyle possible.

Going for gold!

For some reading this, of course, praying together with your husband or wife may not seem likely, possible or, even, something desirable.

If that's the case, we must be careful about saying . . . "I just can't pray with . . .".

However we say it . . . sadly, lovingly or in a mildly condemning way, what we're really saying is that we accept the status quo . . . nothing can change.

We want to challenge that lie because that's what Satan wants us to believe. Everything can change if we begin, in a small act of faith, by asking the Holy Spirit to start to work in us.

If we are committed to being sensitive to each other and are determined to find the 'window of opportunity' when we can pray together, an adventure can begin right here . . .

In prayer . . . in the gifts of the Holy Spirit . . . in trust . . . in togetherness

What remains?

If the chips were down and if we lost every single material possession we own, what alone would remain?

We hope we would be able to say . . .

"It is the richness of our faith in God and the delight in our relationship with our husband or wife."

So let's 'go for gold!' Let's invest in the things that really matter and give praying together a priority in our lives.

We can start to pray together today and, if we used to and we've stopped, don't let's be satisfied until we've started again!

CHAPTER SIX

THE GIFT OF INTIMACY
. . . SEARCHING FOR GOD'S
WILL TOGETHER

Jesus has shown us how much we are loved! Can we doubt that He wants us to enjoy all possible richness and fulfilment in our marriage?

"When we started to pray together it brought us closer together, didn't it?" some newlyweds said to us recently.

When a couple pray together it makes it very difficult for 'separateness' to undermine their relationship. If we take seriously the knowledge that marriages between Christians fail as often as non-Christian ones, it really make sense to use all the resources and grace God makes available to us.

Our marriages are valuable beyond measure and we can choose to take care of them.

"A wedding took place at Cana, in Galilee . . . Jesus had also been invited to the wedding." (John 2:1)

What a difference it makes to share in a wedding day that is graced by the presence of Jesus and is aglow with joy and happiness.

But what of the days/years that follow? Is Jesus still invited?

Mike and Karen Mason make sure they're in touch, they say, *"Love for God and an overwhelming sense of need for his daily help and guidance help us to pray together"*.

Jesus will change our daily water into wedding wine . . . if we ask.

> My love is such that Rivers cannot quench,
> Nor ought but love from thee, give recompence.
> Thy love is such I can no way repay,
> The heavens reward thee manifold I pray.
> Then while we live, in love lets so persever,
> That when we live no more, we may live ever.
> *Anne Bradstreet (1650)*

A journey of discovery

Intimacy – what does it mean? What if either of us, or both, come from families where there was no sharing of hearts, ideas or beliefs in all those growing years? Maybe in your family you talked about the price of eggs or about the latest issue in *East Enders* but nothing much deeper?

Perhaps we've thought of intimacy as a physical, sexual experience but not as one involving the emotions?

The very purpose of marriage, emotional intimacy and companionship, was clearly explained by God's final act of creation, when He said . . . "It is not good for man to be alone, I will make a helper suitable for him." (Genesis 2:18)

In this creative act God's burning concern was to deal with every human being's feelings of aloneness, by giving us a mate with whom we could experience oneness, intimacy and acceptance, and so that we could know the joy and purpose of serving God together.

Here is a blazing description of intimacy in marriage, from *The Mystery of Marriage* . . .

> "*Marriage is about nakedness, exposure, defencelessness, and the very extremities of intimacy. It is about simple unadorned truth between two human beings, truth at all levels and at all costs, and it does not care what pain or inconvenience must be endured in order for the habit of truth to take root, to be watered, and to grow into maturity.*"

Each time Barrie and I read this passage we are spurred on! We really want more of that 'unadorned truth' between us! And we resolve to keep working to bring down any barriers of misunderstanding, gender differences, assumptions and insensitivities that remain.

Pray for each other's needs

Dave and Liz Percival describe very well the process of learning intimacy in prayer.

> "*We are trying to be open with each other on all issues but most importantly trusting each other with our thoughts and judgements on what God is doing in our lives . . .* '

Dave says . . . sometimes we will pray in words, seeking the Lord's will on some matter, or for particular individuals or situation. But at other times we may just sit silently, reflecting in our own ways on what the Lord is saying.

So for us, praying together has been a journey of discovery . . . showing us that we have quite different spiritual gifts. For us 'praying together' is simply a way of describing a journey towards 'spiritual one-ness' that complements our emotional and physical one-ness.

Sometimes we still get it all wrong – I will choose some inappropriate time to share a picture and Liz will analyse and question before the picture is complete or I will resent her clarity and then we end up grumpy and resentful. But when we are sensitive and respectful of our different gifts and gentle in our responses – then we can share in confidence and the Lord can enrich us both."

What does sex have to do with it?

When we talk about intimacy in marriage we of course begin to think about love and sex and we cannot be unaware that we live in a world that has managed to reduce human sexuality to a miserable travesty of what God intended.

"The family is the lifelong opportunity to live for each other. Mutual self-giving the one to the other. What is the relationship between love and sex? In human sexuality it is truly always more than mere sex. Human sexual intercourse becomes more human step by step as a couple become more and more unselfish in their loving."
Dr Victor Frankl in 'Man's Search for Meaning'

As our society engages more and more in the demands of sexual greed, men and women are experiencing unexpected consequences, like increasing levels of impotency and hostility in relationships. Hosts of shattered families and overwhelmed sexual infections clinics (The Commons Health Committee reported a 500% increase in syphilis in past six years. DT 11.6.03) are also some of the more unacknowledged outcomes afflicting us.

But this was God's plan!

Human sexuality was God's design and purpose and His gift to us.

"So God created man in his own image, in the image of God he created him, male and female he created them." (Genesis 1:27)

In the beginning, at the time of Creation, "The man and the woman were both naked, and they felt no shame." (Genesis 2:25) Only after sin had entered into the world . . . "they realised they were naked."(Genesis 3:10) and so they hid themselves from God and, in the process, from each other.

And the truth is that still we hide from each other through feelings of self-consciousness and inhibition in marriage, and in sexual intercourse it is still possible to give our body but withhold ourselves.

Most important to the development of mutually rewarding lovemaking is the understanding that sexual intimacy is God's idea . . . He created it. It is a holy thing and can be understood as a form of sacrament, as an outward and visible sign of the inward and invisible unity or "one fleshness" that God intends us to enjoy in marriage.

This blessing on our sexual intimacy is, of course, completely opposite to the devil's wish to tempt couples to have sex before marriage and then very little after!

A strong affirmation of the purity of married sex comes from the Bible, "Marriage should be honoured by all and the marriage bed kept pure . . ." (Hebrews 13:4). Thus honouring and guarding our lovemaking is our delightful duty and praying together will help us achieve that.

In fact the greater intimacy that many couples discover in praying together can bring new depths to their lovemaking as well as deeper experiences of thanksgiving and worship. A wife expressed it like this . . .

"When he prays with me I feel more intimate towards him and am more likely to want to make love. Equally if I make love to him, he feels more loving and intimate towards me and is more likely to want to pray with me!"

Making the decision to love

Brian and Maureen Devine, who have used their own home to run marriage enrichment courses for over 20 years, recently shared their thoughts on 'intimacy'. Maureen said . . .

"I sat down to pray and sensed there was this enormous gulf, a divide between God and me. I knew it mirrored my relationship with Brian. I also knew that God could and would come in and fill that void, that His Holy Spirit bridges the space in me that is between how I am and how I want to be, if I ask. Just as Jesus bridges the space between Brian and me, when we ask. It is always about making the decision to love, about taking one small step in the right

direction, about reaching out in intimate trust that the other will listen. God works in us through our own efforts. It is all a process of His continuing to transform us into His new creation.

Daily we make sure that we have quiet time before the Lord together. It fulfils a real desire of our hearts, the longing that we have for intimacy with each other and with God. It is our outward expression of His inward Grace, calling us ever deeper into our relationship."

This is how other couples have found praying together has increased their closeness . . .

- We have learnt to be vulnerable to each other by sharing hopes for the future or thoughts and concerns that go deep.

- Together we thank the Lord, acknowledge his presence and commit the day and each other into His Hands.

- We find we understand each other better.

- Prayer brings restoration of unity, through forgiveness received and given . . .

- Knowing how powerful a married couple's prayers are blesses us . . . "When two or three are gathered in my Name, there am I in the midst of them." (Matthew 18:20), and we know He loves to see us praying together.

'Now is the time to deck with flowers'

All that we've written about the value of our joint relationship with God doesn't imply that our *personal* spiritual roots are not important. Nothing can bless our partner more than growth in our own walk of faith. For it would be a tragedy, when the inevitable time comes when we are separated by death, to find we had little relationship with the Lord because we had been relying on the other to be our link to God.

The truth is of course that, whatever our age, we should sometimes think about the certain ending of our marriage partnership in death. We could do no better than to take to our hearts Mike Mason's moving words . . .

> *"Somehow we must learn to mourn our loved while they are yet alive, not waiting until they are gone and our grief does no one but ourselves any good. At least one kiss each day should be watered with tears and planted on bone . . . and love must grapple in advance with remorse, drawing out its sting with little daily acts of tribute. For now is the time to eulogise, now the time to deck with flowers."*
> The Mystery of Marriage

This is how it should be.

Not like the widower, who had been deaf to the heart-felt pleas of his wife before her death, and who was seen after the funeral working hard on the neglected garden and saying, remorsefully, "She would have liked it!"

Growing together

. . . But Jesus said, "Not everyone is mature enough to live a married life. It requires a certain aptitude and grace. Marriage isn't for everyone . . . But if you are capable of growing into the largeness of marriage, do it." (TM Matthew 19:11–12)

THE GIFT OF INTIMACY . . .

The provocative challenge in this verse reminds us where we came in, and asks the impertinent question once more, "Are we grown up enough to fulfil our role in our marriage?"

Our prayer is that, as flawed as we all are, we will each set our face towards the goal of growing *into the largeness of marriage*. That we will experience a fresh oneness with God and each other and that, above all, we will find, in learning to pray together, that our relationship will shed its light into the lives of many.

If you feel in need of some help ... here are TWO PRAYERS to help you begin ...

LORD, we want to begin (or start again) to pray together regularly. We want to open our hearts and our lives to you and to each other. Please help us. We know we can't keep this going by ourselves. Help us to find the right time, the right place for both of us. Keep us determined and trusting in you to make progress. Thank you for the gift of our marriage and for your great, unswerving love towards us. We want to dedicate our marriage to you now. Amen.

LORD AND FATHER, please bless our marriage, help us daily to put each other first and to say, "yes" far more often than we say, "no". We want our marriage to be a blessing to our children (or our friends' children) and to many others. Help us to grow in this coming year in one-ness and wholeness and equip us to support other couples in their relationships. We want to take every opportunity to expand our boundaries and to grow strong together in you. Thank you that life is always an adventure when we walk it with you. Amen.

Reading these prayers out loud together may be all you need to get going. Re-reading (in Chapter 3) on how others have started could also help. Most important of all, don't give up. The Holy Spirit (the Encourager) is always with you.

If your husband or wife does not share your commitment to Christ, you may find that they are willing for you to lead in prayer together each day – even if they are silent. It can become meaningful for you both. If your husband or wife is not happy for you to pray out loud, he or she may be open to you praying silently alongside.

WHEN2PRAY

Barrie and Eileen Jones live just outside of Portsmouth and attend *The Church of the Good Shepherd, Crookhorn.*

They met when both were serving with the Royal Navy. Eileen left the WRNS on marriage to become a full-time mother and for the first 10 years of their married life they were a naval family, after that Barrie taught in secondary schools for twenty years. Eileen was involved in voluntary work supporting family life for 20 years before founding in 1996 the national charity *Positive Parenting,* which is in the forefront of developing resources on parenting skills and in the delivery of training. She was also a founding Trustee of Marriage Resource.

Barrie and Eileen have led marriage enrichment courses for 18 years and are Council members of *One Accord.* They have four adult children who are all married. Their twin daughters both married Americans and now live in Atlanta, Georgia. Barrie and Eileen are much enjoying the fruits of grandparenthood.

Father's Love Letter

The Cry of a Father's Heart from Genesis to Revelation

My Child . . .

You may not know me, but I know everything about you...
Psalm 139:1
I know when you sit down and when you rise up...Psalm 139:2
I am familiar with all your ways...Psalm 139:3
Even the very hairs on your head are numbered...
Matthew 10:29-31
For you were made in my image...Genesis 1:27
In me you live and move and have your being...Acts 17:28
For you are my offspring...Acts 17:28
I knew you even before you were conceived...Jeremiah 1:4-5
I chose you when I planned creation...Ephesians 1:11-12
You were not a mistake, for all your days are written in my
book...Psalm 139:15-16
I determined the exact time of your birth and where you would
live Acts 17:26
You are fearfully and wonderfully made...Psalm 139:14
I knit you together in your mother's womb...Psalm 139:13
And brought you forth on the day you were born...
Psalm 71:6
I have been misrepresented by those who don't know
me...John 8:41-44
I am not distant and angry, but am the complete expression of
love... 1 John 4:16
And it is my desire to lavish my love on you...1 John 3:1
Simply because you are my child and I am your father...
1 John 3:1
I offer you more than your earthly father ever could...
Matthew 7:11

FATHER'S LOVE LETTER

For I am the perfect father...Matthew 5:48
Every good gift that you receive comes from my hand...
James 1:17
For I am your provider and I meet all your needs...
Matthew 6:31-33
My plan for your future has always been filled with
hope...Jeremiah 29:11
Because I love you with an everlasting love...Jeremiah 31:3
My thoughts toward you are countless as the sand on the
seashore...Psalm 139:17-18
And I rejoice over you with singing...Zephaniah 3:17
I will never stop doing good to you...Jeremiah 32:40
For you are my treasured possession...Exodus 19:5
I desire to establish you with all my heart and all my
soul...Jeremiah 32:41
And I want to show you great and marvellous things...
Jeremiah 33.3
If you seek me with all your heart, you will find
me...Deuteronomy 4:29
Delight in me and I will give you the desires of your
heart...Psalm 37:4
For it is I who gave you those desires...Philippians 2:13
I am able to do more for you than you could possibly
imagine...Ephesians 3:20
For I am your greatest encourager...2 Thessalonians 2:16-17
I am also the Father who comforts you in all your troubles...
2 Corinthians 1:3-4
When you are broken hearted, I am close to you...Psalm 34:18
As a shepherd carries a lamb, I have carried you close to my
heart...Isaiah 40:11
One day I will wipe away every tear from your eyes...
Revelation 21: 3-4
And I'll take away all the pain you have suffered on this
earth...Revelation 21:4

WHEN2PRAY

I am your Father, and I love you even as I love my son,
Jesus...John 17:23
For in Jesus, my love for you is revealed...John 17:26
He is the exact representation of my being...Hebrews 1:3
He came to demonstrate that I am for you, not against
you...Romans 8:31
And to tell you that I am not counting your sins...
2 Corinthians 5: 18-19
Jesus died so that you and I could be reconciled...
2 Corinthians 5:18-19
His death was the ultimate expression of my love for
you...1John 4:10
I gave up everything I loved that I might gain your
love...Romans 8:32
If you receive the gift of my son Jesus, you receive me...
1 John 2:23
And nothing will ever separate you from my love
again...Romans 8:38-39
Come home and I'll throw the biggest party heaven has ever
seen ...Luke 15:7
I have always been Father, and will always be
Father...Ephesians 3:14-15
My question is...Will you be my child?...John 1:12-13
I am waiting for you...Luke 15:11-32

LOVE, Your Dad, Almighty God

ABOUT *ONE ACCORD*

The Vision

> ➤ To see thousands of couples living in the love and power of a marriage in Christ.

> ➤ To see teams of couples become effective in supporting marriage and inter-personal relationships.

Our aims

> ➤ To help churches develop a strategy to teach relationship skills and to build teams of couples to support marriage and inter-personal relationships.

> ➤ To equip those couples to become involved in couple support, marriage preparation and mentoring in their communities.

Who we are . . .

One Accord, founded as *Marriage Review* in 1974, is an inter-denominational, nationwide team that currently (2004) comprises about 40 couples; some are teaching couples, some intercessors and there is a small administrative staff. Almost all are volunteers.

In 2003, to reflect our broadening vision, the name of the ministry was changed from *Marriage Review* to *One Accord*.

What we offer . . .

> ➤ Advice (without strings), support and help for churches considering developing a ministry to marriage and relationships.

- Biblically-based marriage enrichment weekends at conferences centres.

- *Time Out for Leaders.* Relaxed midweek or weekend breaks are offered as a free gift to clergy couples and Christian leaders jointly with *The Totnes Family Trust.*

- Leadership of locally organised, non-residential marriage enrichment weekends.

- Flexible, one-day tailor-made events.

- Support to churches in running Holy Trinity, Brompton's 'The Marriage Course', Intimate Life Ministries' Relationships courses and the FOCCUS marriage preparation inventory.

- Prayer support through the scores of couples who pray with us.

When2Pray

Couples Praying Together Initiative

Will you join thousands to support marriage through a great prayer effort that is growing up across the country. Because . . .

> ➢ When we begin to pray, our marriages can bring about huge change, for ourselves and others, because Jesus said, *"When two of you get together on anything at all on earth and make a prayer of it, my Father in heaven goes into action."*
>
> Matthew 18: 19 The Message.

> ➢ God wants to bless and protect our marriages and families.

> ➢ As we look at all that undermines marriage and families today, something very dramatic needs to happen if the younger generation are to enjoy secure marriages and families themselves.

> ➢ Will YOU agree together to be a couple for change and pray together as often as you can for your marriage and for the marriages of others?

> ➢ And will you encourage other couples to do the same?

When2Pray has been written with the endorsement and encouragement of many other national Christian ministries committed to supporting marriage.

They all share *One Accord's* conviction that praying together is of the greatest importance not only to the couples themselves but also for their families and for society at large.

Because lifelong marriage is the healthiest way to live and brings the greatest happiness and security to children, we hope the readers of this book will see themselves as part of a movement of strategic importance, as well as being a part of what we believe the Holy Spirit is saying to His church today.

To help you..

> ➤ 4 Bookmarks are enclosed. Please give them to other couples and encourage them to join in.

> ➤ *When2Pray* – give a copy to another couple!

Order more copies from bookshops, www.amazon.co.uk or

From: One Accord Office
       Market Square, Petworth, West Sussex GU28 0AH
Tel: 01798 345222 Email: admin@oneaccord.org.uk
       www.oneaccord.org.uk

Keep reading . . .

Title	Author
1. ON THE MAGNIFICENCE OF MARRIAGE *The Mystery of Marriage* (Multnomah Books)	Mike Mason
2. PREPARING THE FOUNDATIONS *The Importance of Forgiveness* (Sovereign Booklet)	John Arnott
3. DAILY BIBLE READINGS *Never Alone . . . devotions for couples* (Tyndale House Publishers)	David & Teresa Ferguson
The Word for Today FREE from UCB Freepost ST1135, Stoke-on-Trent ST4 8BR	United Christian Broadcasters
4. ENCOURAGEMENT FROM OTHERS *What Happens when Husbands & Wives Pray Together?* (Spire)	Carey Moore Pamela Rosewell Moore
5. MORE VISION! *Seek my Face* (Roperpenberthy Publishing)	David M Adams
The Lord and His Prayer (T & T Clark)	Tom Wright

6. MARRIAGE SUPPORT

The Marriage Book   Nicky & Sila Lee
HTB Publications

First Year of marriage
The Most Important Year in a   R Wolgemuth & Mark Devries
Man/Woman's Life   S Devries & B Wolgemuth
(Zondervan Publishing)

Learning sexual harmony
Intended for Pleasure   Ed & Gaye Wheat
(Fleming H Revell Company
/Baker Book House)

Relationship insights
Five Love Languages   Gary Chapman
(Northfield Publishing)

Marriage Works   J John
(Authentic Publishing)

Making More of Marriage   John & Ann Coles
New Wine International

When the going gets tough
Loving Against the Odds   Rob Parsons
(Hodder & Stoughton)